Who Put the Spell into Spelling?

This beautifully illustrated storybook has been created to support learners who, after acquiring the basics of reading and writing, have struggled to organically grasp the rules that govern spelling in the English language. The colourful storybook tells the story of the 'Super Spelling School for Letters', and the teacher who helps all the students come together to make words. Twenty-two of the most important spelling rules are explored and given meaning through the engaging story; each followed by a 'quick quiz' to help solidify the rule in the long-term memory. Additionally, there is an activity for each rule which includes reading, spelling and writing in context. This is in the workbook *Supporting Children with Fun Rules for Tricky Spellings* available within this set.

Key features include:

- An engaging story that connects the spelling rules together and gives them meaning, making them easier to remember
- Quirky and colourful illustrations, allowing children to visualise the spelling rules and the way they work in the English language

T0312596

Developed with feedback from teachers and students, this is an invaluable resource for teachers and parents looking to support learners who find spelling a challenge, or who are learning English as an additional language.

Georgie Cooney: I now live in Co Cork, Ireland with 'my family and other animals'. I grew up in North Yorkshire before being 'shipped off' to boarding school and then onto Durham University.

I started my career as a primary school teacher but very quickly learnt that my interest and skills lay in working with learners with difficulties. I think I am able to relate to those who, like me, 'think out of the box'.

I have taught in schools nationally and internationally. Before moving to Ireland, as well as teaching, I trained teachers and adults to work with learners with Specific Learning Difficulties (SpLDs). I gained so much from my students and I keep learning every day. I hope this book set helps you to learn too.

Who Put the Spell into Spelling?

An Illustrated Storybook to Support Children with Fun Rules for Tricky Spellings

Written by **Georgie Cooney**

Illustrated by **Molly Hickey**

Educational Consultant: **Christine Kelly**

Routledge
Taylor & Francis Group

LONDON AND NEW YORK

First published 2020
by Routledge
2 Park Square, Milton Park, Abingdon, Oxon OX14 4RN

and by Routledge
52 Vanderbilt Avenue, New York, NY 10017

Routledge is an imprint of the Taylor & Francis Group, an informa business

British Library Cataloguing-in-Publication Data
A catalogue record for this book is available from the British Library

Library of Congress Cataloging-in-Publication Data
Names: Cooney, Georgie, author. | Hickey, Molly, illustrator. | Kelly, Christine (Consultant), consultant.
Title: Supporting children with fun rules for tricky spellings / Georgie Cooney ; illustrated by Molly Hickey; educational consultant, Christine Kelly.
Description: Abingdon, Oxon ; New York, NY : Routledge, 2020. | Contents: Supporting children with fun rules for tricky spellings activity book--"Who put the spell into spelling?" illustrated storybook.
Identifiers: LCCN 2019043413 (print) | LCCN 2019043414 (ebook) | ISBN 9780367819606 (set) | ISBN 9780367435059 (paperback) | ISBN 9780367819620 (paperback) | ISBN 9781003011040 (ebook) | ISBN 9781003003724 (ebook) | ISBN 9781003011064 (ebook)
Subjects: LCSH: English language--Orthography and spelling--Study and teaching (Elementary) | English language--Orthography and spelling--Problems, exercises, etc.
Classification: LCC LB1574 .C57 2020 (print) | LCC LB1574 (ebook) | DDC 372.6--dc23
LC record available at https://lccn.loc.gov/2019043413
LC ebook record available at https://lccn.loc.gov/2019043414

ISBN: 978-0-367-43505-9 (pbk)
ISBN: 978-1-003-00372-4 (ebk)
ISBN: 978-0-367-81960-6 (Set)
ISBN: 978-1-003-01104-0 (Set) (ebk)

Typeset in VAG Rounded and Avenir
by Servis Filmsetting Ltd, Stockport, Cheshire

Dedication

This is dedicated to Michael Thomas Aloysius Cooney, my adorable dad. His dyslexia meant that he found spellings a challenge in life. Nevertheless, he loved life and life loved him and he successfully made the most of it!

So this is also dedicated to all those people who find that they have to put extra effort into spelling words. It is VERY frustrating so I hope this book set helps you, even if it's just a little bit.

Love from a not-very-good speller,

Georgie

Contents

Acknowledgements

I originally wrote this book in 2006, a long time ago now. I knew then that it was something that could help learners to become better spellers, but I had to see it in practice.

Christine Kelly, a specialist teacher, was instrumental in implementing the lessons over the years and making them fun. More importantly for me, she was able to tell me exactly what worked and what didn't work. She challenged me on a number of occasions and this is exactly what I needed to ensure that this book could reach its objective: to store spelling rules in the learners' memories. She is a wonderful teacher and a brilliant advisor. Thank you Christine.

There were many illustrators who filled a variety of rubbish bins with their ideas and it all seemed a bit hopeless at one point. It was by chance that I saw some Christmas card pictures drawn by my cousin **Molly Hickey**. They were visually brilliant. It was then by good fortune that Molly had the amazing vision that she had.

How does anyone bring an alphabet letter alive? Well, Molly managed it somehow with her fabulous and rare artistic skills and I can't thank her enough.

Joff Brown took a chance on us and shared the vision that we all had for this book. He completely understood what we were looking for and he just put his head down and got on with the task involved. He is clearly a talented and skilled editor.

My spelling guru and my mum, **Mary-Rose Cooney**. Thank you for being a wonderful sounding board and teacher of the English language. You are a skilled grammar and punctuation pioneer!

My husband **Aaron**. A dyslexic who wishes he had had this book when growing up. Thank you for using your amazing dyslexic brain to make this spelling book what it is.

Welcome to *Who Put the Spell into Spelling?*

You are about to find out some of the reasons why we have so many spelling rules in our English language.

There are ridiculous amounts of spelling rules to learn, and they're not all in here, but the most important ones are.

There is a story in this book, which begins in a spelling school for letters. You will see that when you are introduced to the school, it is failing and all the letters are very unhappy. Something needs to be done to sort them out and get them happily working again.

Along the way, you will be quizzed on some important spelling facts. Don't worry, if you're not sure – the answers can be found in the **Parent/Teacher workbook** *Supporting Children with Fun Rules for Tricky Spellings*. You will also find a **glossary** in there for any tricky words you might not recognise.

Furthermore, you will see that with each rule you learn, you will find an activity to do. This is to help the rule go into your long-term memory so that you can remember it whenever you're asked to spell.

It is so hard to remember all the things you're taught in school. That's why this story is here to help you.

We hope you enjoy the story and learning the 22 spelling rules – we couldn't have written this introduction without them.

Have fun spelling!

Letters make words ... but they haven't always made words. They had to go to school to do it, and it took a long time for them to learn how they could spell those words. You will find out how words were made by the end of this story. Letters have names and sounds. Like us humans; we have names but we also make sounds. Their names are said in the alphabet, so let's introduce some of our letters:

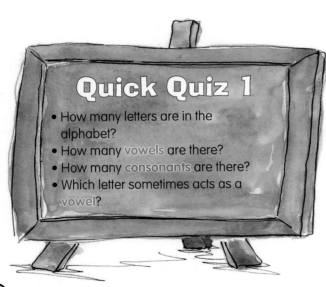

Quick Quiz 1

- How many letters are in the alphabet?
- How many vowels are there?
- How many consonants are there?
- Which letter sometimes acts as a vowel?

Hi! My **long name** is 'soft **g**' as in 'gem'. My **short sound** is 'hard /**g**/' as in 'gate'.

Hi! My **long name** is '**e**' as in 'emu' and my **short sound** is /**e**/ as in 'egg'.

Hi! My **long name** is 'soft **c**' as in 'city'. My **short sound** is 'hard /**c**/' as in 'cat'.

Hi! My **long name** is '**a**' as in 'able' and my **short sound** is /**a**/ as in 'apple'.

There is a horrid, hopeless high school, full of sad, sulking students.

It is called the Super Spelling School for Letters. But it is more repelling than spelling!

FUN FACT

Alliteration is when closely connected words start with the same letter or sound.

For example: **s**tinking, **s**melly **s**ocks!

Quick Quiz 2

- Can you spot the **alliteration**?
- Can you spot the **rhyming** words?

To make words, you need both **vowels** and **consonants**.
The problem is, in the school, the **consonants** and the
vowels do not get on well.

There are always fights on the playground.
No words can be made!

The Headteacher of the Spelling School is petrified that his school will be closed down.

He decides to find a special teacher to help him try and solve his spelling problems.

Miss Magic is a teacher with special powers ... but she doesn't know she has them!

Miss Magic answers the advertisement and she gets the job!

Miss Magic soon learns that nobody is happy at the Super Spelling School for Letters.

The **vowels** seem to be the centre of everything. They think they are the prettiest girls in the school.

They think that they are popular but they are always mean to each other (especially when fighting over **S**, who is the cutest boy in school).

They are particularly unkind to **y**, who is always ignored by them, even though she tries everything to get into their **vowel** group.

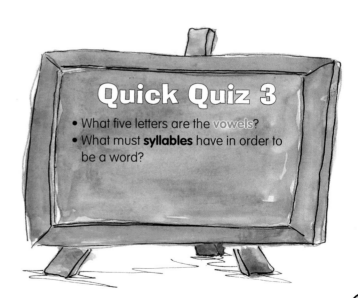

Quick Quiz 3

- What five letters are the vowels?
- What must **syllables** have in order to be a word?

e is the nicest **vowel**.

She is kind and gentle, but the other **vowels** are jealous of her.

Miss Magic has no favourites, but for some reason, when she puts e at the end of words, e makes the other **vowels** say their real alphabet names.

The **vowels** are furious about this and start ignoring e.

Miss Magic tries to change this rule, but it is too late!

Rule 1: Magic E makes the other vowel sounds say their names

Go to Worksheet 2

When **e** is put at the end of a word, it makes the single **vowels** in the word say its alphabet name. e.g. hop**e**.

mat

mate

hop

hope

pip

pipe

tub

tube

When Miss Magic realises that **e** is disliked by the other **vowels**, she tries to make everyone happier by asking **e** to work with some of the **consonants**. So she puts **v** before **e**.

v has a tantrum when he discovers that he has to be followed by **e** at the end of words. So this doesn't help the problem!

Rule 2: V before E at the end of words

Go to Worksheet 3

 comes before at the end of a word ending with a /v/ sound. e.g. grave.

After another argument between the **vowels**, **y** finds **i** in fits of tears.

i is shy and says that she is tired of all the fighting. But worst of all, she is fed up of being put at the end of words and feels lonely.

y, who is gasping for the chance to join the **vowels**, suggests to Miss Magic that she takes **i**'s place at the end of the word. The rule, though, is that she uses **i**'s name.

Miss Magic thinks it is a great idea and **y** is then allowed into the group of **vowels** (but only sometimes).

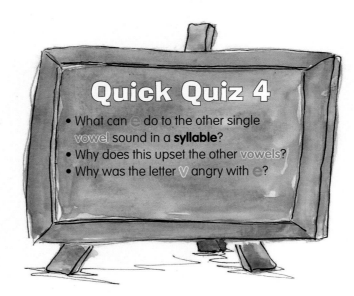

Quick Quiz 4

- What can e do to the other single vowel sound in a **syllable**?
- Why does this upset the other vowels?
- Why was the letter y angry with e?

Rule 3: Y says the name of 'i' at the end of words

Go to Worksheet 4

y can replace 'i' at the end of words or **syllables** but still sounds like i's name.
e.g. my or myself.

cry   try

fly   sly

Miss Magic decides that **y** is doing such a good job of saying **i**'s name at the end of the word that she makes **y** say **e**'s name, also at the end of some words.

- **Noun:** People, places or things. *Horse, stable, saddle*
- **Adjective:** Describes a noun. The *beautiful* horse, the *smelly* stable or the *sturdy* saddle
- **Adverb:** Describes an action. The horse galloped *speedily* and *heroically* across the field

Rule 4: Y says the name of 'e' at the end of words

Go to Worksheet 5

y can replace 'e' at the end of words but still sounds like e's name.
e.g. angry (often seen in **adjectives**, **adverbs** and **nouns**).

happy
clumsily
honey
donkey

Miss Magic becomes increasingly worried that all her hard work is not making things better. The **vowels** are becoming the most hated group in school.

Many of the **consonants** are discovering that they have to change if they follow a single **vowel** sound, so the **vowels** can be protected. The **consonants** are not happy about this.

l, **s**, **z** and **f** have to be doubled after a short **vowel** sound at the end of a **syllable** in words such as cli**ff**, be**ll**, bu**zz**, hi**ss**, e**ff**ort and fi**ll**ing.

Rule 5: Doubling L, S, Z and F after a short vowel sound

Go to Worksheet 6

l, **s**, **z** and **f** double when coming after a short **vowel** sound at the end of a **syllable**. e.g. me**ss**y, fi**zz**ing, hu**ff**ed. These letters are sometimes called 'flossy' letters.

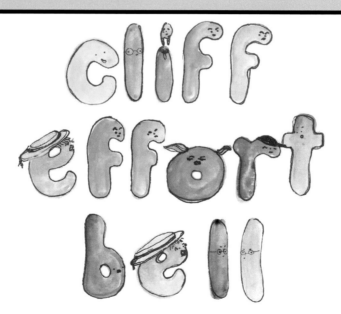

Miss Magic also puts **c** before **k** after a short, single **vowel** sound to protect them at the end of a syllable.

Now **k** is very upset!

Rule 6: C before K after a short vowel sound

Go to Worksheet 7

C comes before K after a short **vowel** sound at the end of a **syllable**. e.g. pick or picking.

Trying to solve the problem, Miss Magic makes **t**, **c** and **h** link up every time they follow a short **vowel** sound at the end of a **syllable**, like ca**tch**, i**tch**, fe**tch** and no**tch**. The short, single **vowel** sounds are angrily wondering why they have to be protected by the **consonants**. Equally, the **consonants** are furiously concerned as to why they have to protect the **vowels**!

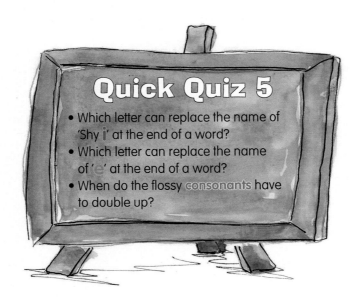

Quick Quiz 5

- Which letter can replace the name of 'Shy i' at the end of a word?
- Which letter can replace the name of 'e' at the end of a word?
- When do the flossy consonants have to double up?

Rule 7: T, C and H after a short vowel sound

Go to Worksheet 8

t, **c** and **h** can go together after a short **vowel** sound at the end of a **syllable**.
e.g. ca**tch** or ca**tch**ing.

To top it all off, angry **h** is furious to find out that he has to follow his enemy **S** after a short **vowel** sound at the end of a **syllable** in words such as da**sh**, fle**sh**, fi**sh**, wa**sh** and pu**sh**.

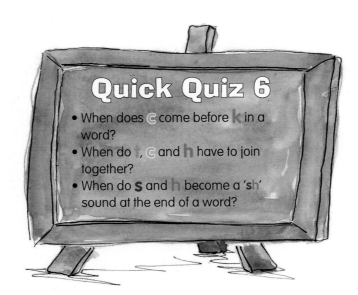

Quick Quiz 6

• When does **c** come before **k** in a word?
• When do **t**, **c** and **h** have to join together?
• When do **s** and **h** become a 'sh' sound at the end of a word?

Rule 8: S before H after a short vowel sound

Go to Worksheet 9

s comes before **h** after a short vowel sound at the end of a **syllable**. e.g. pu**sh** or pu**sh**ing.

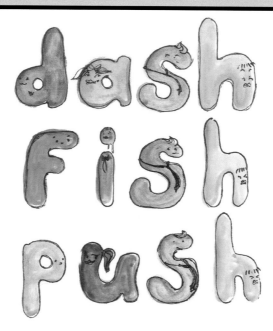

Miss Magic thinks she has found the answer! **S** is added to words to make **plurals** or **verb agreements**, like sock – sock**s**, cat – cat**s**, zap – zap**s**.

Plural means there is more than one. In 'There are many *spots* on his skin', *spots* is a **plural**. In 'He often *spots* problems', *spots* is a **verb agreement**.

However, **S** is confused because his power doesn't work with all words ...

Rule 9: S makes plurals and helps verbs agree

Go to Worksheet 10

S is added to the end of most words to make **plurals** or **verb agreements**.
e.g. many cat**s** (**plural**) or she eat**s** (**verb agreement**).

Miss Magic notices that **e** and **S** have always liked each other. She has a brainwave!

She puts them together at the end of 'hissing' words to make **plurals** or **verb agreements**.

Any words with 'hissing' sounds at the end have **es** added on:

X: box – box**es**
Z/ZZ: buzz – buzz**es**
CH: lunch – lunch**es**
SH: bush – bush**es**
S/SS: class – class**es**

Rule 10: E and S make plurals and help verbs agree (after hissing sounds)

Go to Worksheet 11

e and **S** are added to words ending with hissing sounds like ch, s, sh, x and z when becoming **plurals** or **verb agreements**. e.g. many church**es** or she dash**es**.

Miss Magic thinks everything is solved but she then finds **v**, **e** and **s** are all very annoyed to have to replace **f** when making a word **plural**.

f is not happy either!

leaf – lea**ves**
loaf – loa**ves**
thief – thie**ves**
wife – wi**ves**

Rule 11: F is replaced by VES when making plurals

Go to Worksheet 12

f is replaced by **ves** at the end of words when making **plural nouns**. e.g. leaf/lea**ves**.

leaf
leaves f
grief
grieves f

Miss Magic tries to please the **consonants** by making the **vowels** do more work. She decides to put **i**, **e** and **s** together for words ending in **y** which become **plural** or are **verb agreements**.

copy – cop**ies**
puppy – pupp**ies**
poppy – popp**ies**

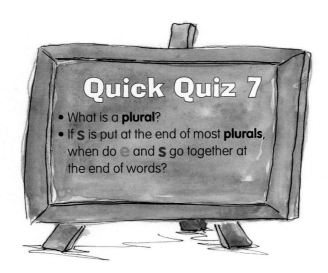

Quick Quiz 7

- What is a **plural**?
- If **s** is put at the end of most **plurals**, when do **e** and **s** go together at the end of words?

Rule 12: I, E and S make plurals

Go to Worksheet 13

y is replaced with '**ies**' at the end of words when making them **plural** and helps verbs agree with subjects. e.g. Halloween *parties* or she *parties* all the time!

Miss Magic tries to make things better by organising a party.

The party is a shambles!

Once the **vowels** realise that  e and **S** are 'together', they are jealous of e and start to throw food at her.

When **S** throws food back at them, the rest of his **consonant** gang follows and there is an almighty food fight!

The party is a disaster and Miss Magic is devastated that it has all gone wrong again.

The Headteacher is not amused.

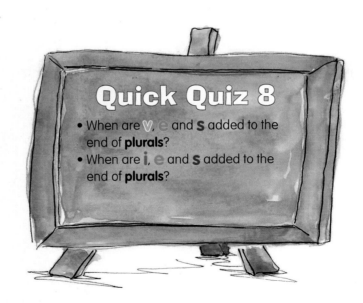

Quick Quiz 8

- When are v, e and s added to the end of **plurals**?
- When are i, e and s added to the end of **plurals**?

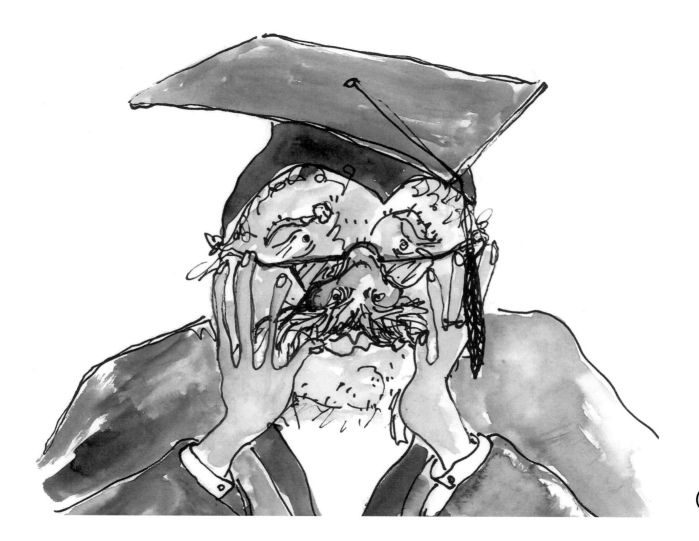

First, the **vowels** are marched into his office and are given a big telling off.

However, the Headteacher finally decides to give all of them as many duties as e.

O's name is now at the end of words such as hello, potato, tomato and halo.

Rule 13: O can end some words

Go to Worksheet 14

The letter name 'O' can end words like hell**o**, potat**o** and hal**o**.

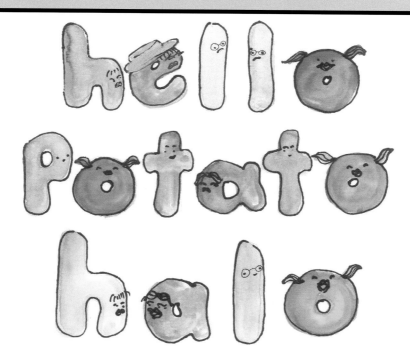

a is to be used on her own before a **noun**, like **a** teacher, **a** school, **a** table and **a** book.

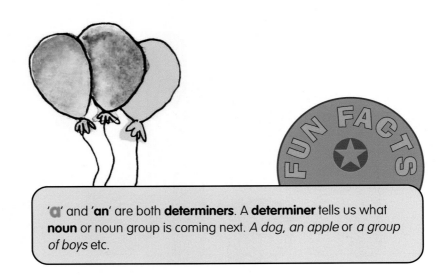

'**a**' and '**an**' are both **determiners**. A **determiner** tells us what **noun** or noun group is coming next. *A dog, an apple* or *a group of boys* etc.

Rule 14: A can introduce words

Go to Worksheet 15

The letter name 'a' can be used as a word to introduce most **nouns**. e.g. a beautiful dress.

However, to avoid upsetting the other **vowels**, **a** is to be joined with **n** before words beginning with **vowel** sounds, such as **an** apple, **an** octopus, **an** elephant, **an** umbrella and **an** igloo.

Rule 15: A and N join together to introduce nouns beginning with vowel sounds

Go to Worksheet 15

a and **n** join together as '**an**' to introduce words beginning with **vowel** sounds.

The Headteacher lets **i** be a capital **I** and a whole word (**pronoun**).

And **i** can come before **e** except straight after **c**.
Like in th**ie**f, ch**ie**f, bel**ie**ve, and ach**ie**ve.

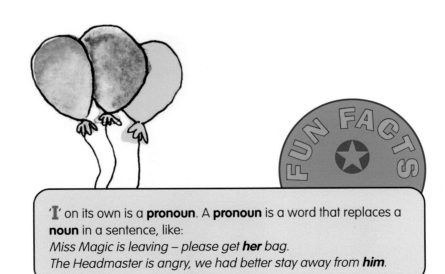

FUN FACTS

'**I**' on its own is a **pronoun**. A **pronoun** is a word that replaces a **noun** in a sentence, like:
*Miss Magic is leaving – please get **her** bag.*
*The Headmaster is angry, we had better stay away from **him**.*

Rule 16: 'I' is a word on its own

Go to Worksheet 16

i can be a word on its own, but it must always be written with a capital **I**. e.g. **I** am tired.

Rule 17: I before E except after C

Go to Worksheet 17

i comes before **e** except after **c** when we hear the '**e**'s name. e.g. re**cei**ve and de**cei**ve.

Miss Magic puts **q** before **u** every time it is in a word such as **qu**iet, s**qu**are and e**qu**al.

Rule 18: Q before U

Go to Worksheet 18

Where there is a **q**, it is always followed by **U**. e.g. **qu**iet or s**qu**are.

The **consonants** are furious because the **vowels** have been given extra powers. To calm them down, the Headteacher tells them that they will have the following powers:

W can change **vowel** sounds in words such as **wa**s, **wo**rld and **wa**rm.

Quick Quiz 9

- Apart from detention, what power did the Headteacher give to:
  The letter **a**?
  The letter **i**?
  The letter **o**?
  The letter **u**?

Rule 19: W can change vowel sounds

W can change **vowel** sounds in words (mainly /o/ and /a/). e.g. w**a**s or w**o**rk.

Go to Worksheet 19

An **irregular verb** is spelt in an unusual way.

†can be used at the end of **irregular verbs** to put them into the past tense – such as slept and crept.

Rule 20: T can change irregular verbs into the past

Go to Worksheet 20

†can change **irregular verbs** to put them into the past tense. e.g. slep† and fel†.

slept

wept

burnt

v can continue to take the place of **f** at the end of a word when that word becomes **plural**, such as:

thief – thie**ves**.

Go to Worksheet 12

Reminder of Rule 11:

f is replaced by **ves** at the ends of words when making **plural nouns**. e.g. leaf/lea**ves**.

leaf

leaves f

grief

grieves f

C is allowed to continue to copy the short sounds for **S** or **k**, so that he is soft in words such as city but hard in words such as car.

(**C** will always be remembered as the Copycat Letter!)

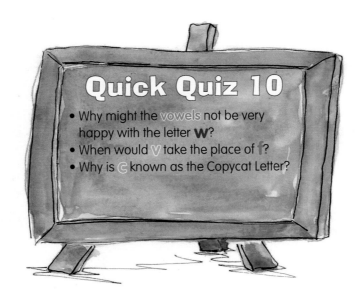

Quick Quiz 10

- Why might the vowels not be very happy with the letter **w**?
- When would **v** take the place of **f**?
- Why is **c** known as the Copycat Letter?

Rule 21: Copycat C

Go to Worksheet 21

C can copy the sounds for **S** (soft c) and **k** (hard c). e.g. city, cent, cycle or cat, cut, cod.

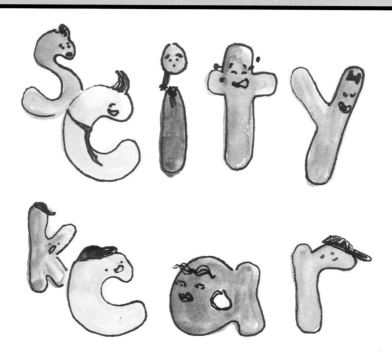

Now **C** can be a 'soft **C**' like city, or a 'hard **C**' like car.

Did you know that '**g**' follows the same rule and can be **soft** or **hard** depending on the letter that follows it? For example, 'gut' is a **hard sound** but 'gem' is a **soft sound**.

FUN FACTS

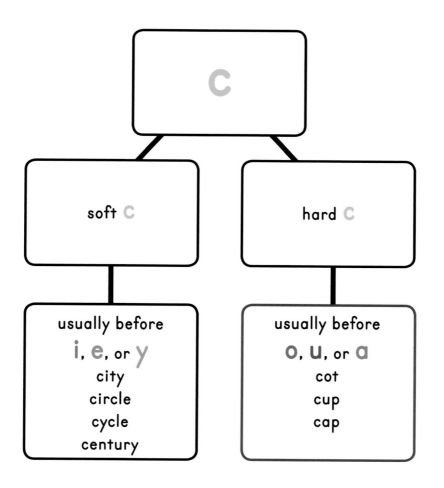

The **consonants** leave feeling very satisfied and they start to make friends with the **vowels**.

y is the last letter to be invited in. The Headteacher tells y that she will have special duties because she is very kind and has always tried to be friends with both **vowels** and **consonants**.

So now you can hear her sound only at the beginning of words such as **y**ellow, **y**o-**y**o, **y**uck and **y**ogurt.

Rule 22: Y's sound comes at the beginning of words

Go to Worksheet 22

Y's sound can only be heard at the beginning of words. e.g. **y**um and **y**ellow.

It is Miss Magic's turn to come into the office. She is very worried.

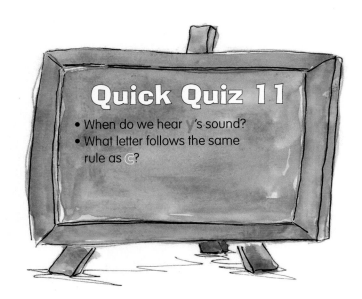

Quick Quiz 11

- When do we hear y's sound?
- What letter follows the same rule as c?

Instead of looking grumpy and angry, the Headteacher gives Miss Magic the most enormous hug! "Thank you Miss Magic, thank you so much!"

"What did I do?" asks Miss Magic with a look of surprise.

"Miss Magic, it was you who put the **spell** into **spelling**!"

Ah, so that's who put the **spell** into **spelling**!

89

Quick Quiz Answers

Page 12 Quick Quiz 1

How many letters are in the alphabet? **26**

How many vowels are there? **5**

How many consonants are there? **21**

Which letter sometimes acts as a vowel? **y**

Page 14 Quick Quiz 2

Can you spot the alliteration? **1) Super Spelling School, 2) horrid, hopeless, high school, 3) sad, sulking students**

Can you spot the rhyming words? **Repelling and spelling**

Page 25 Quick Quiz 3

What five letters are the vowels? **a, e, i, o, u**

What must all syllables have in order to be a word? **A vowel sound**

Page 34 Quick Quiz 4

What can E do to the other single vowel sound in a syllable? **She can make them change their names to their sounds, e.g. cub is changed to cube**

Why does this upset the other vowels? **She has more power than them and it annoys them**

Why was the letter 'v' angry with 'e'? **Again, 'e' has more power than 'v' and has to follow him, even though he is saying his sound at the end of words, e.g. 'live' or 'have'**

Page 42 Quick Quiz 5

Which letter can replace the name of 'Shy i' at the end of a word? **y**

Which letter can replace the name of 'e' at the end of a word? **y**

When do the flossy consonants have to double up? **At the end of a syllable and after a single, short vowel sound**

Page 44 Quick Quiz 6

When does 'c' come before 'k' in a word? **At the end of a word or syllable and after a single, short vowel sound**

When do 't', 'c' and 'h' have to join together? **At the end of a word or syllable and after a single, short vowel sound**

When do 's' and 'h' become a 'sh' sound at the end of a word? **At the end of a syllable and after a single, short vowel sound**

Page 52 Quick Quiz 7

What is a plural? **It means that there is more than one. For example, 1 cat but 3 cats, 1 dog but 101 dogs, 1 book but 3 books**

If S is put at the end of most plurals, when do E and S go together at the end of words? **After hissing sounds like 'ch', 's', 'sh', 'x' and 'z'**

Page 58 Quick Quiz 8

When are 'v', 'e' and 's' added to the end of plurals? **When 'f' is at the end of the singular word and needs to change, for example 'leaf' becomes 'leaves'**

When are 'i', 'e' and 's' added to the end of plurals? **When 'y' is at the end of the singular word and needs to change, for example 'hobby' becomes 'hobbies'**

Page 70 Quick Quiz 9

Apart from detention, what power did the Headteacher give to:

The letter 'a'? **It can be used as word to introduce nouns (a determiner). 'A' can also be with 'n' in 'an' before a noun beginning with a vowel sound**

The letter 'i'? **It can be a whole word on its own when it is a pronoun, for example 'I am called…'**

The letter 'o'? **'o' can now end a word with its sound, for example 'potato'**

The letter 'u'? **'u' has always got to accompany 'q' – I suppose neither of them will ever be lonely!**

Page 76 Quick Quiz 10

Why might the vowels not be very happy with the letter 'w'? **'w' can change the vowel sounds and names however she pleases, for example 'was', 'war', 'work', etc.**

When would 'v' take the place of 'f'? **As we saw in Rule 11 – when 'f' is changing to the plural, e.g. leaf to leaves. It is followed by 'e' and 's'**

Why is 'c' known as the Copycat Letter? **This is because it can make a hard sound like 'k' or a soft sound like 's'. It depends on the vowel that follows e.g. If it's 'a', 'o', or 'u' it's hard as in 'cut', 'cat', 'cot', or if it's followed by 'i', 'e', or 'y', it's soft as in 'city', 'cycle', 'cell'**

Page 84 Quick Quiz 11

When do we hear y's sound? **Only at the beginning of words, such as 'yap' or 'yellow'**

What letter follows the same rule as 'c'? **g**

For Product Safety Concerns and Information please contact our EU representative GPSR@taylorandfrancis.com Taylor & Francis Verlag GmbH, Kaufingerstraße 24, 80331 München, Germany

Batch number: 08244615

Printed by Printforce, the Netherlands